CONDUIT

Rodney —

Thanks for your generosity

Then ks for your generosity

& just so you know I'm not a rinky dink poet

Blessings!

CONDUIT

Khadijah Queen

BLACK GOAT
LOS ANGELES

BLACK GOAT is an independent poetry imprint of Akashic Books created and curated by award-winning Nigerian author Chris Abani. Black Goat is committed to publishing well-crafted poetry and will focus on experimental and thematically challenging work. The series aims to create a proportional representation of female, African, and other non-American poets. Series titles include:

Auto Mechanic's Daughter by Karen Harryman
Controlled Decay by Gabriela Jauregui
eel on reef by Uche Nduka
Gomer's Song by Kwame Dawes

Some of these poems originally appeared in other publications: "Four Suggestions" first appeared in *new ohio review* (spring 2007); "Return via Two Renaissances to a Distinct Unmasking," "Temple of Inscriptions," "Templo de la Calavera," and "Temple XIII" first appeared in the chapbook *No Isla Encanta* (Dancing Girl Press, 2007), along with earlier versions of "Four Suggestions" and "Definitions of Red."

Published by Akashic Books
©2008 Khadijah Queen

ISBN-13: 978-1-933354-51-4
Library of Congress Control Number: 2007908086
All rights reserved
First printing

Black Goat
c/o Akashic Books
PO Box 1456
New York, NY 10009
info@akashicbooks.com
www.akashicbooks.com

To my mother, Denelda,
for her brilliance, wisdom, and strength.

CONTENTS

INTRODUCTION

Conduit, Khadijah Queen's debut collection, is itself a current that runs through a historical and mythical past, continuing through our troubled present. These stunning meditations seem to be engendered by a "bruising in the earth." The poems in these sequences are called up out of the soil and already belong to us before we come to them. Her landscapes awaken from our unfolding ecological and anthropological devastations and serve as offerings to a conquered body that cannot be separated out from its own dwelling.

There persists for Queen the "uncharted resilience" of the body. The brilliance of these poems resides in their ability to accommodate the complexity and disappointments of events like Hurricane Katrina ("The flood wide open — ") without denying the passage of time or the distances we hold before and after any moment in time. "How we do know we work" writes Queen in a question that holds its statement and a statement that holds its question. We "Shrug, / drift off," she writes. Hers is a poetic sensibility that denies the poem transcendence and conclusion. The water that makes up the body and the earth's surface will continue to flow forward in time and this fact is akin to the rhetorical power that moves us through this collection: *"Be glad that more than once / You can break."*

Conduit, with its insistence on the marriage between a "downward suspicion" and an "uncharted resilience," evolves into not a bruising in the earth but a definition for humanity. The beauty of the language and precision of the gaze transform into a spirit that remains present.

Claudia Rankine
March 2008

/ DISTANCE AS THE ROOT
OF OLIVE TREES /

For our struggle is not against flesh and blood . . .

—Ephesians 6:12

FOUR SUGGESTIONS

—for ariel r.

i. */Indifference/*

You could drift off.
        A downward suspicion,
Making surreptitious curves.

You (I am not willing)
Lost a figure of instance, yesterday. Figured
        Secretly
            I declined

To go further than this. That I would have
(Had to)
        Come at a time different, more unlocked than—

❋

/But this is where I stop and start, no more/

This stance which is no mechanical habit.
A reflex

Stoked irregularly
       Into the shape
       Of a conquered spine. Not willing I have
                  Yet conquered
This, earned this
       Particular scrutiny.

But this is where I stop and start, no more.

      ✤

ii. */Demarcation: as in: to isolate/*

      I'll not
      Couple overlook with hints
      At catastrophe.

—And how will you arrive?

      Averted or
      Otherwise.

     Wearing four heliotrope
     dresses in a single afternoon.

❊

/Wild shifts of sunlight cold and night/

Four heliotrope dresses,

A single afternoon

I wear whole and all —

(*I have counted the thousand thirsty buds*
burrowed in the black
bulk of your loosened
hair)

✶

iii. /*Capitulate: as in: a rapid apprehension*/

Crawl inside the anxiety of neglect.

Disregard
  Postures arranged
  Bone on bone.

Think: blood swelling muscle.

✿

/Or: unnatural clicks/

And jibes cells of neglected bodies
Endure. In the name of.

Shaken by lack of disturbance.
(Interior menaces
Winking their mysterious processes,

How we do know we work —
Why guard?)   Be conquered.

Shrug,
            drift off.

❋

iv. */To depart further/*

Insinuate, if an act.
I am not willing:

      Offer then auxiliary
Signals to supplement circumstance, compound elements,

Synchronize events within our secreted
Imbalances.

—*Did we create?*

     ✿

/Uneven theft, a likely
            Wave/

A score of
Fluid acts, unused

        Indications. Conceive of patterns

Concurrent with another's want:

        (Manners demand—
        Looking down.)

                ❉

/With a body willing to lie still on the surf, to be covered
Only in what waves will carry/

Andamos —

At the balloted beach, private tides
        Funnel into borrowed caves —

    And what have we found there?

More consecutive kinds of submission.

     ❄

/Pitched elements choosing
   A shrouded resting place/

Under the grainy veil of sand,
   Tell me —

What did happen?

   (An accident of proof.)

A simple fix, some sun, some rock —

   The whole point is to sink. To know

(No isla encanta,
   It interfered —)

   To know what runs through.

   ❋

DISTANCE AS THE ROOT OF OLIVE TREES

/5:22 a.m./

Suffer your cherished distance, wound like cord;
You'll not give yourself away.

You hear people on the streets braced for loss, and inside us

Another frozen universe   is cracking.

❊

/A water-locked asylum,
Red-black on the inside/

On a terrace overlooking olive trees at dawn,

Think of olive oil in a mother's work-hardened hands.
Her desperation

    To soften them. Her young child's face
Turning away.

✶

/7:19 a.m./

Somewhere in these ancient groves:

      All the shadows you've ever meant to cast.
You would prefer to collect them
             Like this:

Standing at a window the length of a wall,
While white curtains inhale

      The breeze, then   exhale onto your bare thighs.

❈

/Self-portrait at noon/

Often, the largesse of your uncertainty
                    Restrains your doubled features.

           Territory or persona, a landscape like you
Juts toward unkind impulse,

           Assumes an underground holiness.

✤

/Cultivar/

Above the bony talus, gnarled branches drip ripe
      Green drupe, unpicked.
You watch strays lap the sour, swallow.

        Inviting healing, cut figs
On your table tonight, pale-sweet,
      Become wished fruit, a provocation.

✳

/4:24 p.m./

There is an endlessness
Guarding the wrecked shell of your body.

The strings of your muscles thrum
       A song tattooed in your inky throat.

An unexpected sequence, like abandonment
Spreading

Into the shadow of a cheekbone,
The gut of a lock —

       ✻

/Be glad that more than once
You can break/

Absence:

A way to make an overturned bowl of the sky.

❀

/Survey/

The burden of course
    Is everything you didn't want:

Nerves that pin the body
    To itself. The sudden need to cross

Agreed-upon thresholds:

    The mind is a bell-shaped road
    ringing back.

❋

/Midnight/

How then
　　　　To slow down your own obscenity, construct it
　　　　　　　A small camber, grafted freely —
　　Sense upon countered sense —

One root　　　cannot seem to rest next to another; like meek

Alluvial women, traveling between their work of knowing and
Not, posing,

Making a fog of external surfaces,　　　an odyssey of each
　　　　　　　　　　　　Hollow fluctuation —

　　Such distance is not meant to be ingested.

❋

/Tomorrow/

East is a crashed line of heaven,

A row of dusty lanterns.   The west shore, half-lit with wreckage.

The rare filigree —

A name not taken away, but resigned.

❁

/On the way to the Pyrenees, 2006/

Summit-bound,
  You might expect   a little violence now and then.

           Step among the hard, rising curves of wood
                Bruising in the earth, bruising earth.

Watch the sandpiper lean and stretch, the returning *agiopouli*
                Speak in the sleek mode of entitlement,
           Shed acuity of the offered body,

     Ticking off the miles, the minutes,

Their wings stretched apart,
Like this.

        ❁

CURRENT

/A break in the line of foam/

Do not follow the rip current.

If you must, draw down
Your best formalities—a brackish wink,

Your wave-perched mass,
Orbital arms;

See they do not wear out.

✸

/Reasons not to drown/

Of course, fingerprints do not
Evaporate if a woman somewhere

Soars horizontally out to sea.
But how not to

Seize the oscillation, dive under,
Fearless, no longer blind
To parallels.

❀

/Calm yourself/

Think past the present.

Ignore the erupting chaos,
    Cobalt waves pulling you

From shore. Do not look at your hands

    And think you can cull
Immediacy.   Swim toward everything

    You cannot see,
The calculated axis, portions of you

    Spinning,
        A conduit.

❋

/ OFRENDAS ROJAS /

LA KATRINA

Unravel your hurts at night.
        Unfurl them, sacred flags,
        And hoist them
        Above your body, of course

You are alone.
        Even when another's breath
        Guides yours, glides
        Airily into you, you are alone.

Believe there is only one.
        Accept it as the most
        Forgotten of all truths.
        Even in the arms

Of marigolds, one. Of course
        You are alone. Unravel
        Your hurts at night.
        Hoist them, little postcards

Against a blooming sky.
        Count them
        As they float back down,
        Cover you,

Fold them and tuck them
      Like kisses under your skin
      Like masks of afternoon,
      Tender as the leaves of limes.

Of course you are alone.
      There is no mercy
      Except that which you grant yourself.
      Even alone, even at night,

Your body covered in *cempoalxochitl*,
      In the thriving pain
      That has unpacked you,
      Tricked you, turned you

Inside out, there is no mercy
      Except that which you grant
      Yourself. Unravel your hurts at night,
      Your body singing black *corridos*.

✵

FLOOD

/After, a sea of marigolds/

Take divided blooms,
Sew them in a bustled
      Dress,   wear it to *Mictlan,*
Petals dancing at your feet

      Eat nothing but *rosquete*   *hojaldra* —
Bread to swell the vacant belly

      Embrace *calaca* with a fervent tongue,

Like *Chalchiuitlicue* receive
      The flood wide open —

      Take divided blooms,
Sew them in a raft of red,
Pet *Izcuintle* in your awful sleep
      Make it to *Tlalocan*
Weeping, and thirsty.

❂

TINCTURE

Be my *curandero*.
Make me crushed
   Marigold teas

That I may swallow a respite—
Esta ofrenda es una limpia,
   Temazcal,

Ritual for the starved
   And worthy.

   ✿

TEMPLE OF INSCRIPTIONS

/We'll not climb easily up the ruined steps/

Only hours before we lay whole.
We lay whole in the way these hills do, breezes

Drifting across the surface disturbing nothing —
No, *bahlam kin* — the sleeping jaguars start to move.

❂

TEMPLO DE LA CALAVERA

/When you came to Palenque you did not know/

Stars could enter the body, but for the roof one could enter
The vast, brash cradle of sunset.

You wished to put your hands into the eyes of stone skulls,
As if to render smooth palms rough and holy.

✳

TEMPLE XIII

/Cinnabar, Zinjifrah, originally meaning "lost"/

Perhaps the Red Queen fell in love with death.
In her hollow middle room,
Cochineal red,
Mercury with sulfur spice dusting her bones,
A chemical praise
Hard (or soft) as a fingernail,
As the thought that beauty is enough,

Praise is enough, as the thought that names
Do not matter —
Only malachite, jade diadems,
Human sacrifice, obsidian
Blades for the afterlife.

❖

DEFINITIONS OF RED

What hues lie in the slit
When a mask breaks
          —Hayes (Lorde)

i. */Red as a means of encroachment/*

A ruby stain
On the edge of a collar,
      A swapped dress, smoothed smile—

Tempered skies, made sudden,
Darkening with each doomed cloud

      Without warning, white packs dripping into
Tourmaline darkness
          Which let them go—

      Let go presumptions of height,
Of depth, left this zealous rain: expectant leaves

      Boil to a crisp nothing,
Helpless, offering not a seam of skin,
Not a knuckle not a vein.

❁

ii. */Core/*

A red cloud is a hymn of descent,
A string of red *guindillas*,
A crushed cloud-heart.

Red for red:
Deep lines in curved palms.

A birdstone lathed in blood.
A shift in the span of continents.
Covet the faltering weight.

❀

iii. */Degas red:*

    Three ballet dancers/

Intruded, finally, exquisitely so —

    With a red that lies outside the shoulder blades,

Red stroked over boned fabric

        (A ballet of red ghosts),

Taut skin stitched inside

    A loose-skirted garment

    (Praise the now-widened heart),

So she is erect but uneven:

    The neck is
    red, like a blush.

        ✿

/And what of their hands/

Three incomplete hands,
      Fingers never divided, never fully drawn,
Or else in shadow, a trinity,
            Closed, open, high and fisted —

      But a fourth, unseen, amputated by position;
The strip of the dancer's bodice, a cap of hair,
        Tulle, lace hint her; not so her blank face —

✿

/Not so the browned-out face, not absent but a function/

Unluckily or intentionally
    Becomes the shaped space
Between the crook of another woman's elbow and bitten lip,
          Sketched in, scratched out —

Yet the light under the red dancer's chin, the soft white light
On what must be the chest of the faceless,

        Suggested one, so strategic; a swipe of light
    For her, *and here I thought the hand must be working*
       Against the hidden dancer's breast —

✿

/ SUSPENSION TACTICS /

EASY

Answer your own questions.

      Think of how he encompasses you,
      The small moon he has made

Of your mind. To say nothing of

The body, attenuated
Fastenings that started it all,

      The temptation to tease, to flank,
      Feign capture.

             ✻

PROLIX

The mouth, above all things, knows how to smother.

Knows well
The body's lethal contour, its useless constraints,

Its sometime triggers
        Knitting snatches of memory

Into offbeat tragedies,
Regional ellipses, easily fabricated

Affairs —   marginalia
        Gone reckless, gaudy, lowly wrought —

The mouth: a failed schemata of inlets.

A grate full
Of graffito. Indelicate

Mouth, prone to extractive
            Penalties — of both fairness, and a tendency

    To condemn, to ease into liminal withholding,

Unchecked breath in each syllable falling toward decay.

WAYS TO UNSETTLE THE FLESH

—for naomi b.

/Remote preparations/

Invent the lives
    Behind each kempt landscape.

Flowering, like graves, on a hillside,
Ideals impossible to finger.

False premonitions,
       Stunned-still instants, each one
The chasm of a furious kiss.

And voice is a brushful
Of red ochre. Warm, untidy
Pitch. Worth the joy in keeping.

            ❊

/Between silt and structure/

The delusion of naming
A thing meant to be used—

    Grateful to be of use:
Its interceding plot lines a graying calendar
(Above and beneath, an altered
      Continent of dying. Flesh,

Its visible almanac) tucked close to the lungs,
Pages wide and vibrating—

    ✻

/An unmaking/

Distance, in the body, is made whole,
Transformed from void to dwelling place.

Its maze of history as
Twisting as that of an olive tree,

Its grooved flank, firm leaves
Leaving traces of shadow.

The love it must have taken
Not to let it be cut down.
   The uncharted resilience.

   ❋

/Diatonic/

The bulwark that is
  A man, hiding himself.

  Observe,   *without modulation,*

An acute biologic adherence: his
   White notes

Scrape your thinning ear
  Perfect, poached as ivory, lying

Underneath and around the black keys
Of an old piano, yellowing

  At every practiced touch.

    ✤

/With a minimum of care/

Hold this pattern together.

Be the who one asks, *Who*
          Have I not thanked enough for this?

De verdad, I have
Meant to be uttered, gently, from the mouths
               Of those I love, yet stroked and stark

As a craving, circled
In lilts and groans,

Slim crests of silence
          Slivered between.

❋

/With dead stars (as grafted onto the fixed remnants of)/

Compose a prophecy of performance.

Show me again the way sex blows city smoke at twilight,

Draws diagrams of ligaments, capsules of jasper-flecked hair
      Swaddled in a conch shell,

          Makes fists of loose nebulae,

      Eyefuls of infrared spirals.

            ❊

/Add shelter   nearer plot
Than faith/

Walk the shifting
Streets midnight to sunrise, imagining violets
       Lie in the chinks of every corner.

Collect wedge leaf,
       Hooked spur, sharptail, creeping root—

By daybreak, consume
     The fragrant, wild-stemmed whole:

     Risk all reason for vigilance.

      ❀

SUSPENSION TACTICS

/Espéralo/

Your god was a god that waited.

Nestled in the eternal unclaimed,
    Praised for attending the isolato, a god

      You breathed a certain love into.

Denied the timed days of your life, listen:

      He swore only to *a combination of things* —
    Secret affiliations, scotoma,

      The color black, the color blue.

      ✳

/Traga el pantano/

Every day see yourself without.

   Desire unmoored from its greedy tether.
Shrinking, lovely,

   Each shamed part of you
That never surrenders.

   Wait for signs of return.

      ❊

/Espéralo,   al lado de las estrellas envenenadas/

Find a way to dream him
  Out of unconscious manipulations,

   To yield instead

A prized emblem
  Sans rules and measures,

Torn from the plush
  Altar of someone else's future god,

A decadent totem
Poised for the stirring of small miracles.

     ✿

/Todos los días, queda en la espera/

An expert in such things,
        You don't believe in escape.

        Take witness,

Stand on a bed of cloud, a sky of this—

                    ❋

/Tenga paciencia en su prisión/

Engage in accidental acts of rapture.

    Seize each polluted hour,
    Allotropic, ruthless:

We do not guess
    How you have paid.

            ❧

RETURN VIA TWO RENAISSANCES
TO A DISTINCT UNMASKING

/Santa Maria Novella, 14^b c./

When she asks what you've seen, you say:
"Shadow. Firenze is full of shadow."

You've never been to Italy,
But declare undying love for da Firenze's *ballata* —

You love the idea of voice as an instrument, that two
Is not two, but dissonance.

❁

/Romeo & Juliet, etc./

ools: stopwatch, hacksaw,
An electric blower from your hidden
Overgrown shed. It's in the wrist—

The hammer, dear, the nails,

Perfect cuckolds.   Frames you've made
Of kind brutal grins.

The corners sharp, reaching,

Each side strained against the other.

✻

/Evolution of maestros & madrigals/

You are obsessed with legends of the trecento,

Drawing on rocks with chalk, swearing
    Your life, too, swung
Toward cathedrals—

        God through
The quickening transference:

    "Art is a leap through time."

    ✻

/Interruptions/

Not shy, but hushed, she asks, "Love me

In Italian." You trace *amare*
Onto her bare, radiant shoulder,
The buds of your fingertips leaving

    A trail of heat,   tears
As heavenly favor.

        ✧

REFERENCES

"La Katrina," "Flood," "Tincture," and "Temple XIII" (Based on Mayan architecture, mythology, and present-day Mexican rituals derived from Mayan, Aztec, and other Mesoamerican Indian practices—i.e., *Día de los Muertos*)

> *Calaca*—grim reaper
>
> *Cempoalxochitl*—marigold
>
> *Chalchiutlicue*—goddess of water/consort of Tlaloc (god of rain and floods)
>
> *Curandero*—spiritual healer, shaman
>
> *Izcuintle*—small dog that guides the dead to the underworld
>
> *La Katrina*—Lady Death
>
> *Limpia*—ritual cleansing
>
> *Mictlan*—lowest (ninth) level of the underworld
>
> *Red Queen*—an unnamed woman, likely royalty, her skeleton covered in cinnabar, buried in Palenque's Temple XIII
>
> *Rosquete, Hojaldra*—two types of sweet bread, beautifully decorated, often in the shape of bones
>
> *Temazcal*—traditional sweat bath for spiritual cleansing
>
> *Tlalocan*—layer of the underworld reserved for those who have drowned

"Return via Two Renaissances to a Distinct Unmasking"

> *Andrea da Firenze*—leading composer of *ballate*, d. 1415 (also, Lorenzo da Firenze, teacher & composer; Gherardello da Firenze, known for madrigals and *ballate*)
>
> *Ballata*—a secular musical form during the trecento (13th to 15th c.), or Italian *ars nova* period

ACKNOWLEDGMENTS

Many thanks to the following people, whose love, support, and insight helped to make it possible for me to write this book:

Naomi Benaron, Mary Brown, ariel robello, and Beth Pietrzak—consummate readers. Thank you for lending your incisive minds and your precious time.

My sisters Kim, Taliah, and Vanessa; my son Tariq; and my friends and family—Natasha Marin and Ashaki Jackson; Veatrice Pettygrue; Makeda Smith; Tiffany Bradley. Thank you for your generosity and encouragement.

Mom—thank you for your capacity for giving and loving unselfishly; Dad and Grandma—thank you for the gift.

Chris Abani—thank you for guiding me to this path.

Other selections in Chris Abani's Black Goat poetry series

GOMER'S SONG
poems by Kwame Dawes
72 pages, trade paperback original, $14.95

"As someone who professes to be a writer, I'm struck dumb by Kwame Dawes's pinpoint and devastating lyricism and the unflinching assurance of each and every stanza. These gems, threaded with mesmerizing narrative, exhibit both unbridled imagination and a lean technical mastery . . . This is the kind of work writers strive for. This is Dawes at the pinnacle of what he does."
—Patricia Smith, author of *Teahouse of the Almighty*

AUTO MECHANIC'S DAUGHTER
poems by Karen Harryman
84 pages, trade paperback original, $14.95

"In her debut collection, Harryman presents poems that celebrate small moments of love and life and showcase her extraordinary dexterity with words and image. She creates something profound out of the ordinary and reminds readers of the singular even in the mundane. Her syntax is lovely, and her poems offer a subtlety that is truly wonder-filled."
—*Library Journal*

CONTROLLED DECAY
poems by Gabriela Jauregui
136 pages, trade paperback original, $15.95

"This first collection marks a new mind terrain, radical tempos, and wild-style tropes in Latina Letters and all poetry today—breaks through with incredible caliber and impossible power. She is Hegel and Kahlo, Serpent and Zen, Cantina blade and Zapatista jungle."
—Juan Felipe Herrera, author of *187 Reasons Mexicanos Can't Cross the Border*

"Jauregui displays perfect pitch: Her lyrics are impressive in their scope, range, empathy—and especially their authentic passion."
—Marjorie Perloff

eel on reef
poems by Uche Nduka
152 pages, trade paperback original, $15.95

"Nigerian-born Nduka's poems in *eel on reef* are more about image than sense . . . [and] there is much to appreciate in his joyous language, his percussive rhythms; his sense of movement runs like a river through pages with no titles and limited punctuation."
—*Library Journal*